WordWork Book

Volume 1, Units 2–8

Cambium
LEARNING®
Group | Sopris

Printed in the United States of America
Published and Distributed by

4093 Specialty Place • Longmont, Colorado 80504
(303) 651-2829 • www.soprislearning.com

Contents

Unit 4 I Can

Unit 5 Tap and Kick

Unit 6   **The Big Fish**

Unit 7 | Hip-Hop

Unit 8   Zapcat Fan

Create *jam*

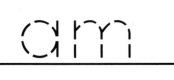

_____ am _____

_____ _____

_____ jam _____

_____ _____

Sam is in a _____.

Name _____

Create *ram*

_____ a m _____

_____

_____ r a m _____

_____

The _____ is in the jam.

Name _____

Making a Word Web

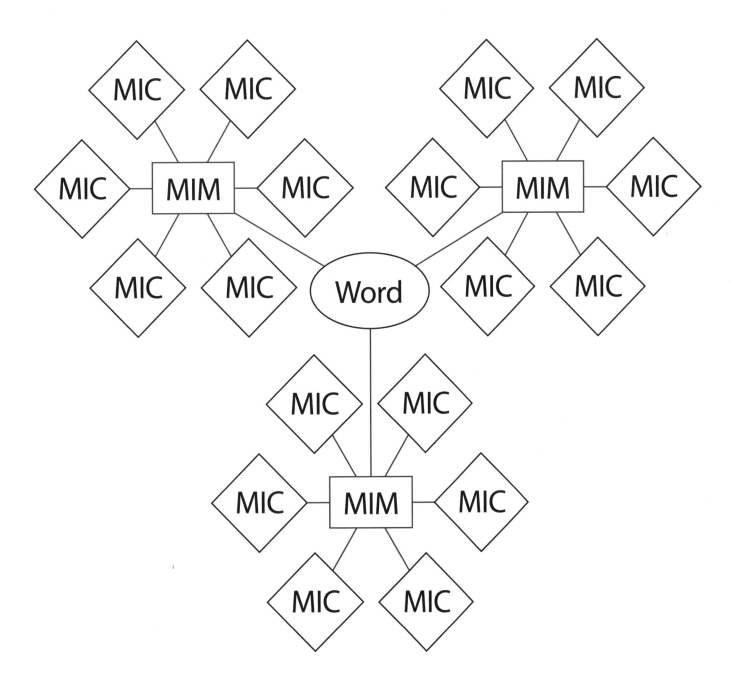

Create *lap*

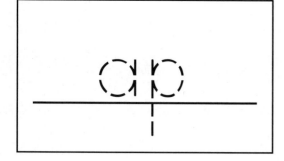

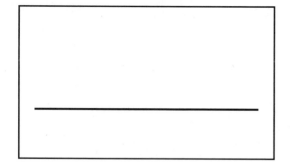

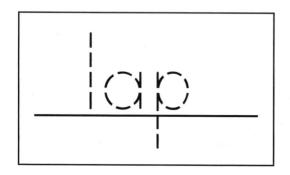

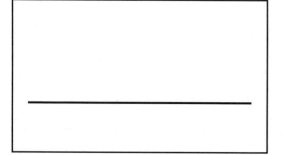

2.3.a

2.3.c

2.3.d

The cat is in my _____ .

Create *tap*

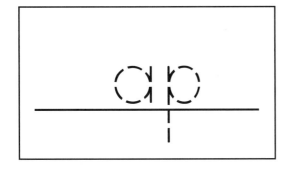

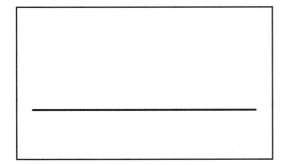

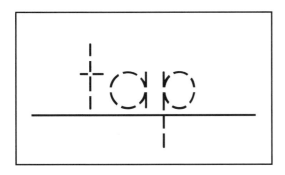

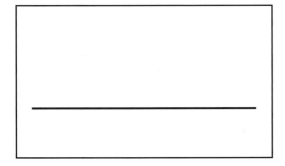

_____ it, Sam.

Eye-Spy Words

_____

_____

_____

_____

_____

_____

_____

_____

"Tap the Jam"

Tap, tap, tap…

tap the jam.

Tap, tap, tap…

tap the ram.

Tap, tap, tap…

tap the lap.

Time taken:

1st reading _____   2nd reading _____   3rd reading _____

am and *ap* Rime Family Words

am

_____

_____

_____

_____

_____

_____

_____

ap

_____

_____

_____

_____

_____

_____

_____

Name _____

Writing Core Words and Rime Family Words

_____

_____

_____

_____

_____

_____

_____

Name _____

Boxing in Core Words and MICs

Write a word (from the Image Card).   Write or draw a MIC.

_____

_____

_____

RAN Chart

ram	lap	jam	lap
tap	ram	lap	tap
ram	lap	tap	jam

Time taken:

1st reading _____   2nd reading _____   3rd reading _____

"The Ram and the Jam"

This is Pam.

Pam has jam.
This is Sam.

Sam has a ram.
The ram is in the jam!

Sam!
Sam is in a jam!

Time taken:

1st reading _____   2nd reading _____   3rd reading _____

Name _____

Create *bat*

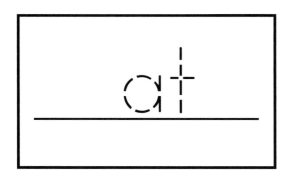

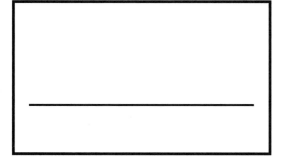

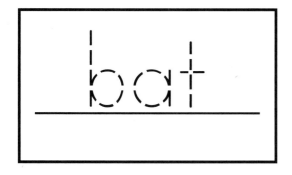

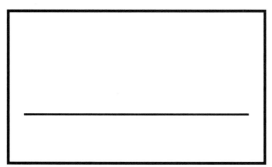

This is a _____.

Name _____

Create *pat*

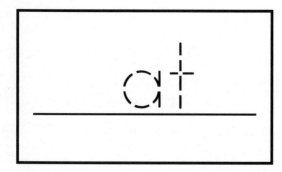

3.2.a

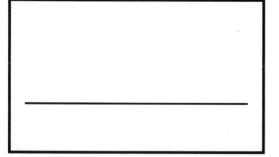

3.2.b

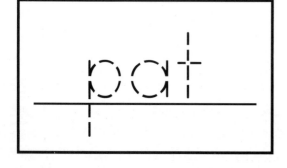

3.2.d

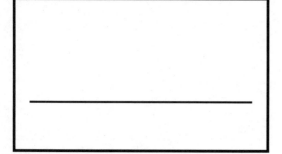

Do not _____ a bat!

Name _____

Dictated Phrases *bat* and *pat*

1. _____

_____

2. _____

_____

3. _____

_____

Name _____

Create *ham*

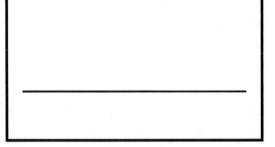

3.3.c

3.3.a

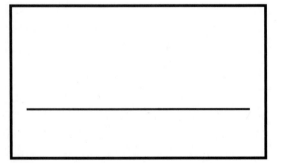

3.3.b

Pat is a _____ .

Name _____

Create *tag*

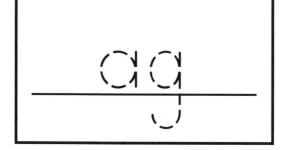

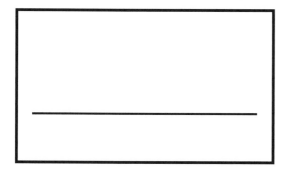

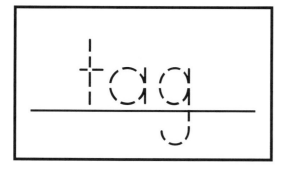

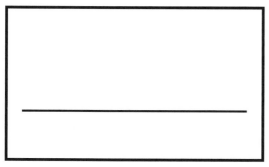

3.4.a

3.4.b

3.4.c

The cat has a _____.

Name _____

Dictated Phrases *ham* and *tag*

1. _____

_____

2. _____

_____

3. _____

_____

Name _____

Rime Family Words

Starters: _____   **Rimes:** _____

Real Words	Non-Words

Name _____

Eye-Spy Words

the
is
in
a
this
and
has

_____

_____

_____

_____

_____

_____

"The Bat"

This is a bat.

This is a fat bat.
The fat bat is a ham!

See the fat bat in the cap?
See the tag on the cap?

This is Sam.
Do not pat a bat, Sam!

Time taken:

1st reading _____   2nd reading _____   3rd reading _____

Name _____

Ender Bender s

laps

bat

ham

jams

tap

rams

tags

Name _____

"At Bat"

Bat it, Pam!

Pam bats it.
She tags the bag.

Tap it, Sam!
Sam taps it.

Matt tags Sam.
Zap it, Pat!

Pat taps his cap.
Pat zaps it!

Time taken:

1st reading _____   2nd reading _____   3rd reading _____

Name _____

Ender Bender Worksheet

Write the words below with Ender Bender **s**.

Core Word	Ender Bender	Core Word + Ender Bender **s**
ham		
bat		
tag		
jam		

Name _____

"Tag the Ham"

Pam has 3 hams.

Pam has 3 tags.
Pam tags the hams.

Sam sees his tag and his ham.
Sam jams his ham in a bag.

Sam taps his cap.
Sam is happy.

Time taken:

1st reading _____   2nd reading _____   3rd reading _____

Name _____

RAN Chart (Core Words)

ham	tag	pat	bat
tag	bat	ham	pat
bat	tag	pat	ham

Time taken:

1st reading _____   2nd reading _____   3rd reading _____

Name _____

RAN Chart (Core Words + Review)

bat	ham	lap	pat
tap	ram	tag	bat
ham	tag	pat	tap

Time taken:

1st reading _____   2nd reading _____   3rd reading _____

Name _____

Nouns and Verbs Worksheet

1. Matt tags Sam.

2. Pat taps the bat.

3. Pam bags a ham.

4. Sam taps his cap.

5. Pam tags the hams.

6. Matt jams!

Name _____

Boxing in the Rimes

_____ am	_____ ap	_____ at	_____ ag

_____	_____
_____	_____
_____	_____
_____	_____

Name _____

Create *can*

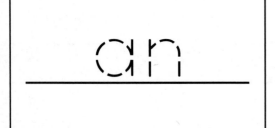

4.1.b

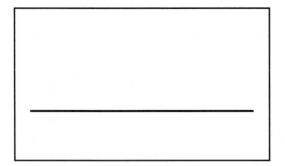

4.1.a

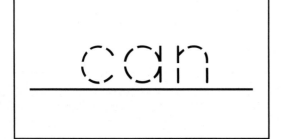

4.1.c

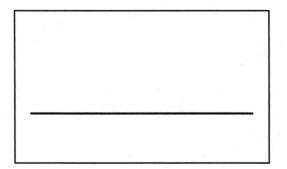

The _____ is in the bag.

Name _____

Create *fan*

_____ an _____

_____

_____ fan _____

_____

4.2.b

4.2.a

4.2.d

I can _____ the man.

Name _____

Dictated Phrases *can* and *fan*

1. _____

_____

2. _____

_____

3. _____

_____

Name _____

Create *cap*

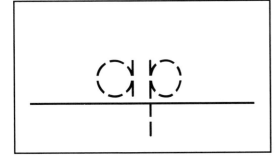

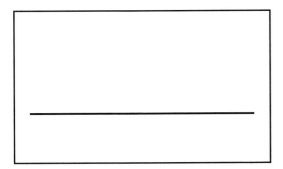

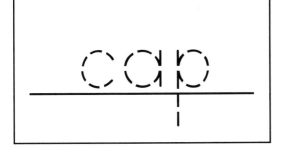

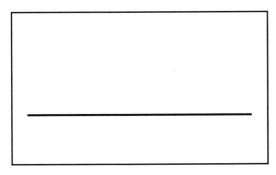

4.3.a

4.3.b

4.3.d

The fan taps his _____ .

Name _____

Create *pad*

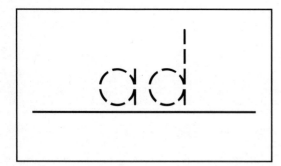

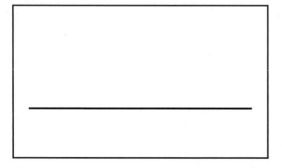

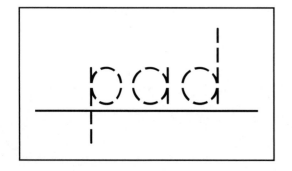

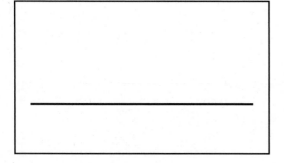

4.4.d

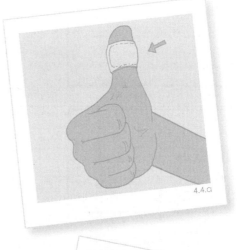

4.4.a

4.4.e

The man has a _____ .

Name _____

Dictated Phrases *cap* and *pad*

1. _____

_____

2. _____

_____

3. _____

_____

Name _____

Eye-Spy Words

the	do
is	on
in	not
a	see
this	at
and	it
has	she
	his
	happy

_____

_____

_____

_____

_____

Name _____

"I Can"

I can tap.

I can nap.
I can cap it.

I can map it.
I can fan a pan.

I can fan a man.
I can jam it in a van.

I can jam it in a can.
I can can-can!

Time taken:

1st reading _____   2nd reading _____   3rd reading _____

Name _____

Rime Family Words

Real Words	Non-Words

Find the Rime Pattern

A cat sat on the cap.

The ham is in the can.

The man is in a jam.

The ram laps from the tap.

Pat is a fan of Pam.

Pat is mad at Sam.

Pam will tag the hat.

Name _____

Words Using Double Trouble and *ing*

1. _____

2. _____

3. _____

4. _____

Name _____

"A Fan Can Fan"

A bat can bat!
The bat bats!

A ram can ram!
The rams are ramming!

A fan can fan!
The fan is fanning Pam.

A bat fans!
It is fanning the man.

Jam can jam!
The jam is jamming.

The ram in a cap is batting.
He has fans.

Time taken:

1st reading _____   2nd reading _____   3rd reading _____

Name _____

RAN Chart (Core Words)

cap	can	fan	mad
can	mad	fan	cap
fan	cap	mad	can

Time taken:

1st reading _____   2nd reading _____   3rd reading _____

Name _____

Ender Bender Worksheet for Paired Activities

Choose the word that fits in the sentence and write it in the space.

Pam is _____.

bat
batting
bats

· ·

Pat is _____ his cap.

taps
tap
tapping

· ·

Sam _____ it.

tap
tapping
taps

· ·

The ram is in a _____.

jamming
jam
jams

Name _____

RAN Chart (Core Words + Review)

cap	fan	ham	bat
tap	pat	cap	ham
bat	can	fan	tap

Time taken:

1st reading _____ 2nd reading _____ 3rd reading _____

Name _____

Create *tip*

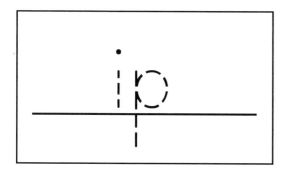

5.1.b

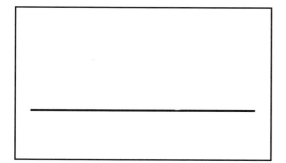

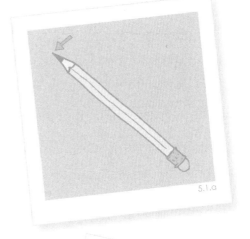

5.1.a

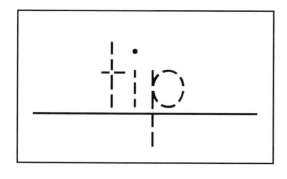

5.1.d

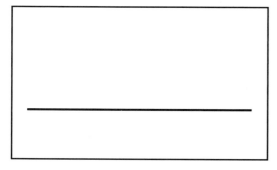

See Bill _____ his hat.

Name _____

Create *dip*

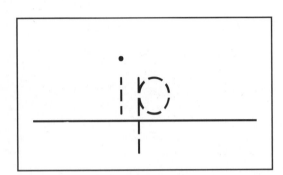

5.2.a

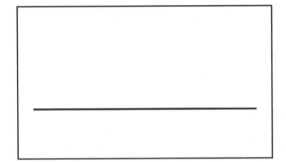

5.2.d

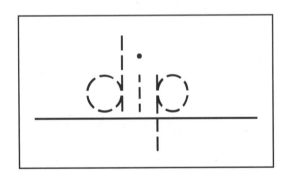

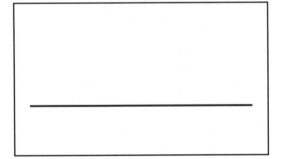

5.2.e

Pat and Jan _____ ham in the jam!

Name _____

Dictated Phrases *tip* and *dip*

1. _____

_____

2. _____

_____

3. _____

_____

Name _____

Rime Family Words

Real Words	Non-Words

Name _____

Create *bit*

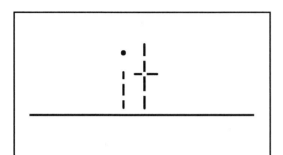

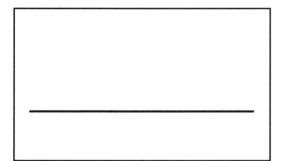

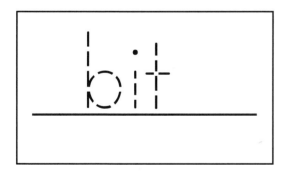

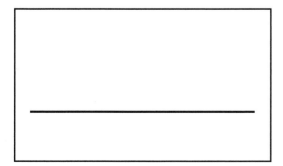

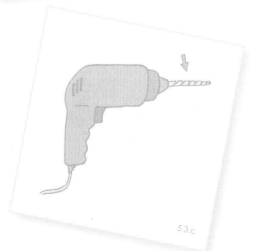

Dan has a _____ of ham.

Name _____

Dictated Phrases *bit* and *sit*

1. _____

_____

2. _____

_____

3. _____

_____

Name _____

Create *bill*

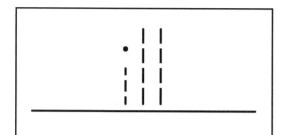

5.4.a

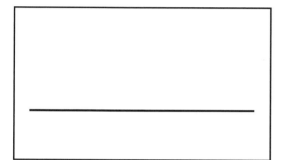

5.4.c

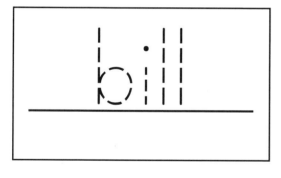

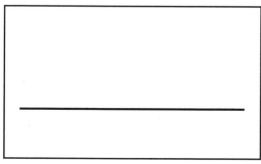

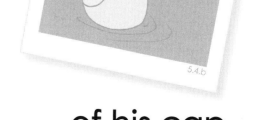

5.4.b

Will taps the _____ of his cap.

Name _____

Dictated Phrases *bill* and *fill*

1. _____

_____

2. _____

_____

3. _____

_____

Name _____

Create *kick*

_____ick _____

_____

kick _____

_____

Sam can _____ it.

Name _____

Dictated Phrases *kick* and *pick*

1. _____

_____

2. _____

_____

3. _____

_____

UNIT 5

Name _____

Eye-Spy Words

the	do	I
is	on	are
in	not	
a	see	
this	at	
and	it	
has	she	
	his	
	happy	

_____

_____

_____

_____

_____

"Tap and Kick"

This is Nick.
Nick can tap and kick.

Nick can tip and dip.

Nick can tap the bill of his cap.
He can kick the tip of a can of dip.

This is Bill.
Bill will tap and kick a bit.

RIP!

Bill will sit.

Time taken:

1st reading _____   2nd reading _____   3rd reading _____

Name _____

Rime Family Words

Real Words	Non-Words

Name _____

"Dan Can"

I am tapping. Can Dan tap?
Dan taps.

I am kicking. Can Dan kick?
Dan kicks.

I am fanning. Can Dan fan?
Dan fans.

I am tipping. Can Dan tip?
Dan tips!

I am napping. Can Dan nap?
Dan naps.
Shhhh…

Name _____

Ender Bender Worksheet

Core Word	s	ing	ed
kick	kicks		
dip			dipped
bill		billing	
fan			fanned
tip		tipping	
bit		✕	✕

Name _____

Writing Ender Bender Words

Choose one rime pattern and one Ender Bender to form a word. Watch out for Double Trouble!

Rime Patterns:

___ am ___ an ___ ick ___ ip

Ender Benders:

_____ s _____ ed _____ ing

1. _____

2. _____

3. _____

4. _____

5. _____

6. _____

7. _____

8. _____

Name _____

"The Ram Kicked"

The ram sees the can by the man, and he kicks it.

The can tips, and a bit of dip hits the bill of the man's cap.

A bat nips the bit of dip! The man with the cap is not happy.

He fans his cap at the bat.

The bat dips and rams the ram. The ram is not happy.

Time taken:

1st reading _____   2nd reading _____   3rd reading _____

Name _____

RAN Chart (Core Words)

bill	dip	kick	bit
kick	bill	bit	tip
bill	bit	dip	kick

Time taken:

1st reading _____ 2nd reading _____ 3rd reading _____

Name _____

RAN Chart (Core Words + Review)

dip	kick	cap	bag
bit	bat	bill	dip
fan	cap	bat	bag

Time taken:

1st reading _____   2nd reading _____   3rd reading _____

Name _____

Create *dig*

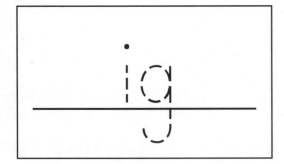

6.1.b

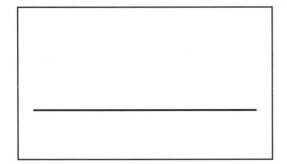

6.1.a

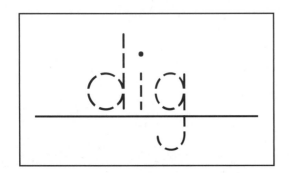

6.1.c

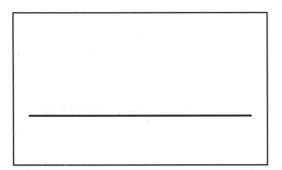

I will _____ for it.

Name _____

Create *pig*

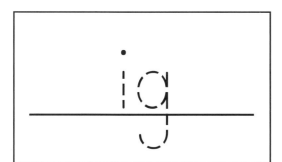

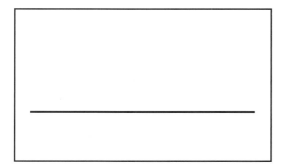

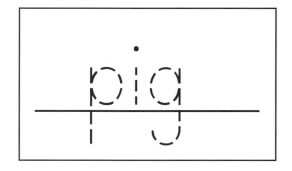

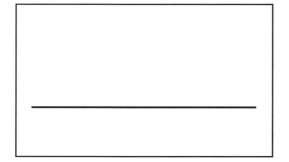

The _____ is big!

Name _____

Dictated Phrases *dig* and *pig*

1. _____

_____

2. _____

_____

3. _____

_____

Name _____

Create *fish*

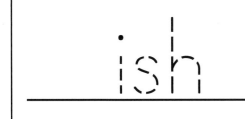

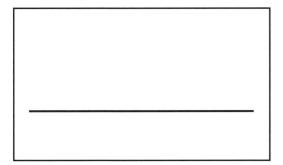

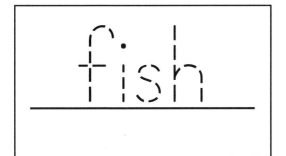

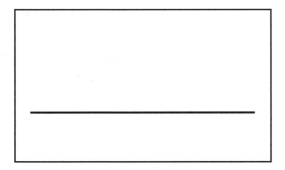

I wish for a _____.

Name _____

Dictated Phrases *fish* and *dish*

1. _____

   _____

2. _____

   _____

3. _____

   _____

Name _____

Create *pin*

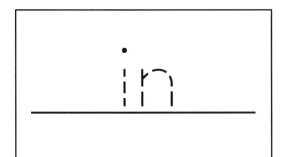

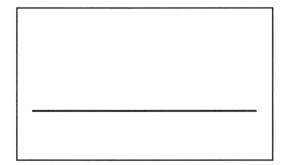

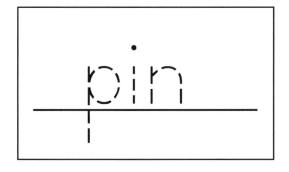

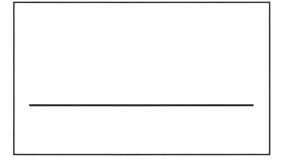

I will _____ it on the cap.

Name _____

Dictated Phrases *pin* and *fin*

1. _____

_____

2. _____

_____

3. _____

_____

Name _____

Create *kid*

id
_____

_____

kid
_____

_____

6.5.a

6.5.c

6.5.b

She is a big _____.

Name _____

Dictated Phrases *kid* and *lid*

1. _____

_____

2. _____

_____

3. _____

_____

Name _____

"The Big Fish"

This is Bill.
Bill is a big kid.
Bill is a big kid with a big fish.

This is Jill.
Jill is a bit of a kid.
Jill is a bit of a kid with a big fish.

Nip, nip! The big fish bit Bill on the hip.

Jill kids Bill.
Will Bill win the pin?
Will Jill win the pin?

Jill wins the pin!
The man pins the fish pin on Jill.
Jill digs it!

Time taken:

1st reading _____   2nd reading _____   3rd reading _____

Name _____

Rime Family Words

Real Words	Non-Words

Name _____

Eye-Spy Words

the	do	I
is	on	are
in	not	of
a	see	he
this	at	by
and	it	with
has	she	
	his	
	happy	

_____

_____

_____

_____

_____

Name _____

"A Kid Can Fish"

A kid can fish for a big fish.
A kid can wish for a big wish.
A kid can wish for a big fish.

A kid can pin.
A kid can wish for a fish pin.

A kid can dig.
A kid can dig in a big dig.

Can a kid fish, wish, pin, and dig?

Can a pig fish, wish, pin, and dig?
I am kidding!

Time taken:

1st reading _____ 2nd reading _____ 3rd reading _____

Name _____

Ender Bender Worksheet

Core Word	s	ing	ed
fish	fish		
pin			pinned
kid		kidding	
dig			×
bill			billed
pig			

"Nick at Bat"

Nick can kick and tap and bat.

This is Nick at bat with his big bat.

This is his batting cap. Nick is tipping the cap a bit to his fans.
He is kidding the fans.
The fans dig Nick.

Nick is tapping and digging in.

Nick is batting. It is a big hit.

Can Bill tag Nick?

Bill is mad. Nick did it!
The kids win.

Time taken:

1st reading _____   2nd reading _____   3rd reading _____

Name _____

Diagnostic Writing Activity

Rime Pattern

[ ]

Rime Pattern

[ ]

[ ]

[ ]

[ ]

[ ]

[ ]

[ ]

[ ]

[ ]

[ ]

Name _____

RAN Chart (Core Words)

dig	pig	fish	pin
kid	fish	pin	kid
pig	dig	fish	kid

Time taken:

1st reading _____   2nd reading _____   3rd reading _____

Name _____

RAN Chart (Core Words + Review)

pin	kid	kick	tip
fish	dig	tap	pin
cap	fish	pig	kid

Time taken:

1st reading _____   2nd reading _____   3rd reading _____

Name _____

Rime Family Words in Lesson 1

Real Words	Non-Words

Name _____

Create *rock*

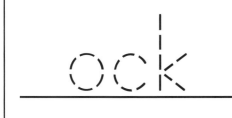

_____

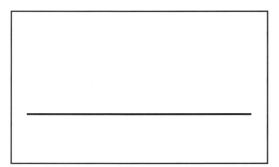

_____

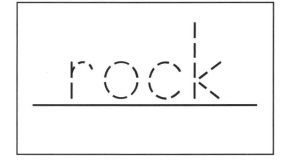

_____

_____

Uh-oh! This _____ is _____ing.

Name _____

Create *lock*

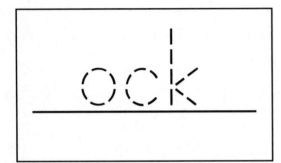

7.2.c

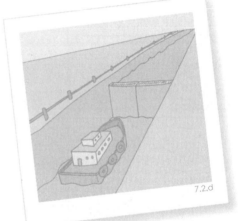

7.2.d

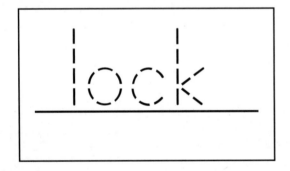

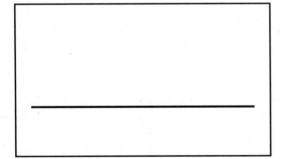

7.2.e

Nick _____s his _____ .

Name _____

Dictated Phrases *rock* and *lock*

1. _____

   _____

2. _____

   _____

3. _____

   _____

Name _____

Create *pot*

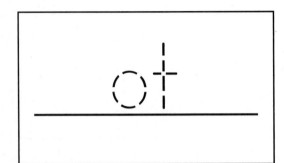

_____ot

_____

p͟o͟t͟

_____

Dan _____s plants in this _____.

Name _____

Dictated Phrases *pot* and *hot*

1. _____

_____

2. _____

_____

3. _____

_____

Name _____

Create *bob*

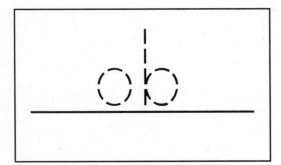

7.4.c

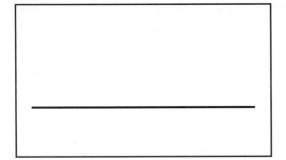

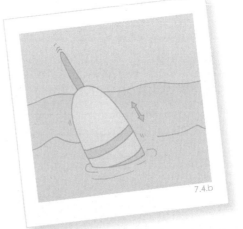

7.4.b

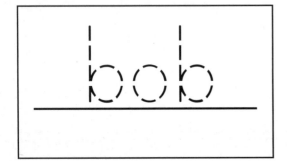

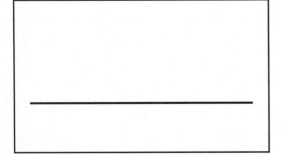

7.4.a

Pam's _____ cut _____ed as she ran.

Name _____

Dictated Phrases *bob* and *rob*

1. _____

_____

2. _____

_____

3. _____

_____

Name _____

Eye-Spy Words

the	do	I
is	on	are
in	not	of
a	see	he
this	at	by
and	it	with
has	she	for
	his	to
	happy	

_____

_____

_____

_____

_____

Name _____

"Zapcat With the Man in the Van"

I am a man.

I am a man with a cap.

I am a man with a cap in a van.

I am a man with a cap in a van in a jam. I am mad in this jam.

I am Zapcat. I am with the man in the van.

The man in the van said, "Zapcat, I am a fan!"

Time taken:

1st reading _____ 2nd reading _____ 3rd reading _____

Name _____

Picture Drawings

Box 1

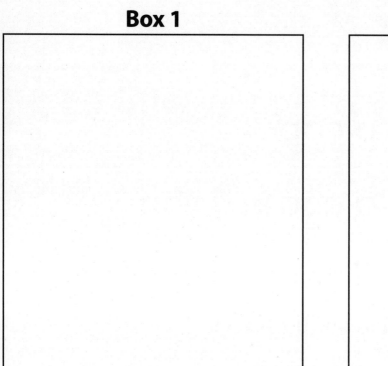

Box 2

Box 3

Box 4

Name _____

Create *top*

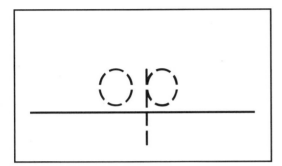

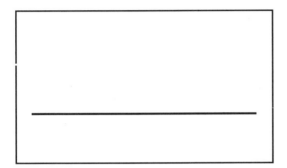

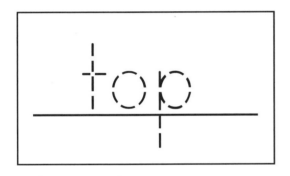

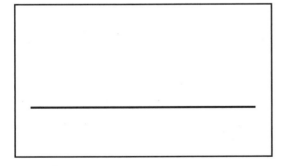

7.5.b

7.5.c

7.5.e

Bob hopped to the _____ of the rock.

Name _____

Create *pop*

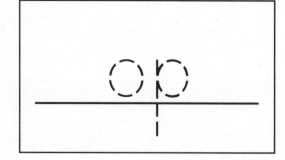

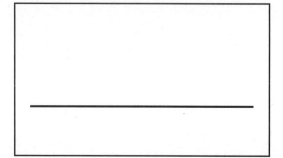

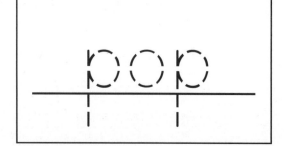

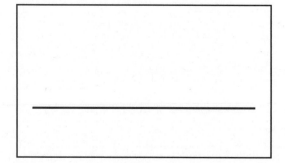

7.6.a

7.6.e

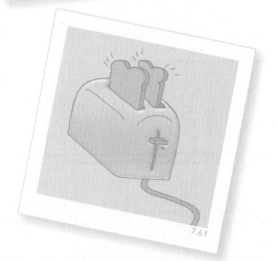

7.6.f

_____ sips _____ from his mug.

Name _____

Dictated Phrases *top* and *pop*

1. _____

   _____

2. _____

   _____

3. _____

   _____

Name _____

Ender Bender *er* Words

_____

_____

_____

_____

_____

_____

_____

Name _____

"Hip-Hop"

Nick can tap and kick and rap.

Bill rocks and hops and jams.
Bob pops in and raps and jams.

The kids dig hip-hop and pop.
Pop gets a kick from the jamming kids.

Hip-hop rocks!

Time taken:

1st reading _____   2nd reading _____   3rd reading _____

Name _____

Fatrats Challenge Word List

Zapcat

catnap

ragtag

madcap

laptop

catfish

bobcat

tiptop

Name _____

Fatrat Words

_____

_____

_____

_____

_____

_____

_____

Name _____

"The Wishing Rock"

Pop sat on the rocks, and the kids sat with him. Pop had a rock. He said, "My pop had lots of rocks. He had rocks in pots and rocks in socks."

"He had little rocks locked in a locker."

"Pop had his top rock in the top of his locker. It was his wishing rock. If he tapped the rock, he got his wish."

The kids said, "Can we pick a wishing rock?"

What will the kids wish for?

Time taken:

1st reading _____   2nd reading _____   3rd reading _____

Name _____

Rime Family Words in Lesson 5

Real Words	Non-Words

Name _____

RAN Chart (Core Words)

top	lock	rock	pot
pop	bob	top	rock
pot	pop	lock	bob

Time taken:

1st reading _____ 2nd reading _____ 3rd reading _____

Name _____

Dice Rime Family Words

Real Words	Non-Words

Name _____

Ender Bender Words

Core Word	s	ing	ed	er
pop		popping		
bob			bobbed	
pot	pots			
rock		rocking		
lock	locks			
top				topper

Name _____

Rime Pattern Selection

1. The man _____ the can.
   [tips, tops, tap]

2. The ham is in a little _____.
   [pot, pit, pat]

3. The fish is _____ on the rocks.
   [jammed, jimmed, jommed]

4. Bob can _____ and kick a bit.
   [hap, hop, hip]

5. Pat sat on my _____ and had a story.
   [lop, lip, lap]

6. The _____ is in the cap.
   [tog, tag, tig]

7. I lock my pin in my _____.
   [licker, locker, lacker]

8. The _____ has _____ the van.
   [ribber, rabber, robber]   [tipped, topped, tepped]

Name _____

"The Top Cop"

Bob is a top cop.

He hopped from his van and locked it.
Bob hopped to the top of the rock.

Rocking, rocking, a madcap robber
tipped the van.

The robber popped the lock and
robbed the van.

Bob got to the van. Bob pinned the
robber to the van.

Bob got the robber to admit that he
robbed the van.

Bob is the top cop at his job.

Time taken:

1st reading _____   2nd reading _____   3rd reading _____

Name _____

RAN Chart (Core Words + Review)

ram	dip	bill	pop
rock	kick	pot	ham
bob	top	lock	fish

Time taken:

1st reading _____ 2nd reading _____ 3rd reading _____

Name _____

er Sentences

Add *er* to the word in ( ) to make a word that makes sense. Then write the word on the blank line.

1. What is the _____?

   (mat)

2. He is the _____.

   (bat)

3. This is _____.

   (bit)

4. The pig is _____.

   (fat)

5. She sat in the _____.

   (rock)

6. The kid goes _____ _____.

   (pit)   (pat)

Name _____

Rime Family Words in Lesson 1

Real Words	Non-Words

Name _____

Create *nut*

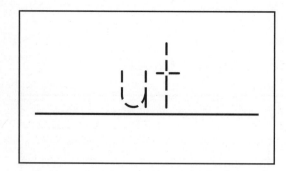

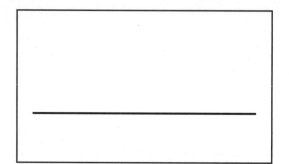

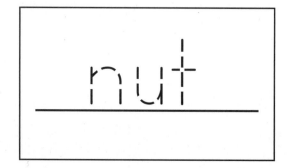

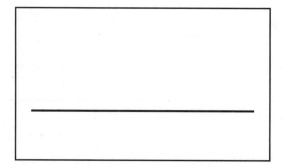

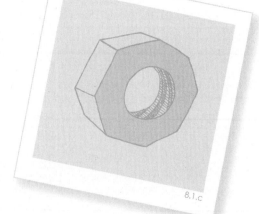

I am a ham and jam _____.

Name _____

Dictated Phrases *nut* and *hut*

1. _____

_____

2. _____

_____

3. _____

_____

Create *bug*

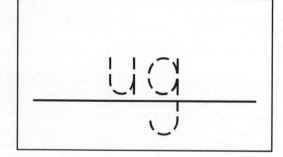

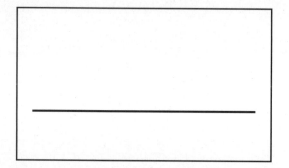

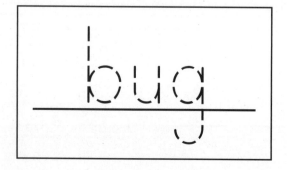

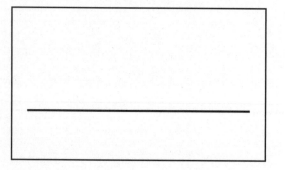

8.2.b

8.2.a

8.2.c

Do not _____ me!

Name _____

Dictated Phrases *bug* and *rug*

1. _____

_____

2. _____

_____

3. _____

_____

Name _____

Rime Family Words in Lesson 2

Real Words	Non-Words

Name _____

Create *run*

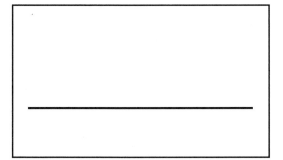

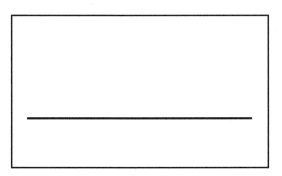

Go and _____ the tub.

Name _____

Dictated Phrases *run* and *fun*

1. _____

   _____

2. _____

   _____

3. _____

   _____

Name _____

Create *duck*

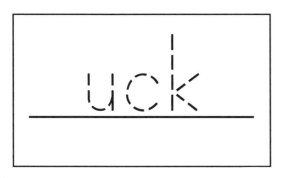

8.4.a

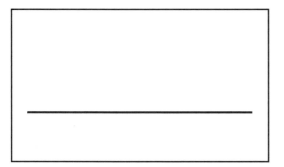

8.4.b

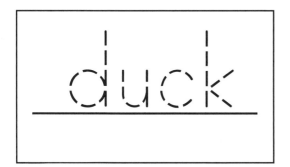

8.4.c

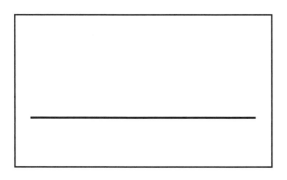

The _____ bobs and dips.

Name _____

Dictated Phrases *duck* and *luck*

1. _____

   _____

2. _____

   _____

3. _____

   _____

Name _____

Eye-Spy Words

the	do	I	get	that
is	on	are	from	
in	not	of	what	
a	see	he	my	
this	at	by	was	
and	it	with	little	
has	she	for	him	
	his	to	we	
	happy	said	if	

_____

_____

_____

_____

_____

Name _____

"Zapcat Fan"

This is the man in the van.

The van is in a big rut.

The man is cut.
This is bad luck.

Zapcat!
Zapcat runs to the van.

Zapcat tugs and tugs on the man in
the van.

The man in the van hugs Zapcat.
"Zapcat, I am a big fan."

Time taken:

1st reading _____   2nd reading _____   3rd reading _____

Name _____

Create *rub*

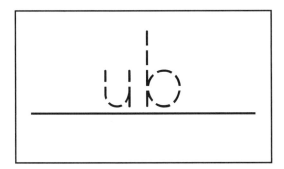

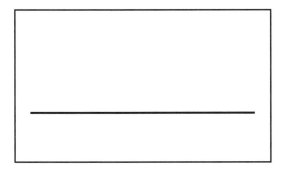

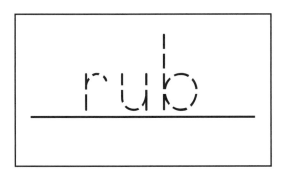

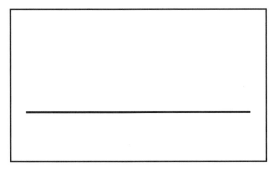

_____ the rock for luck.

Name _____

Dictated Phrases *rub* and *tub*

1. _____

   _____

2. _____

   _____

3. _____

   _____

Name _____

Create *just*

_____ ust _____

_____

_____ just _____

_____

8.6.a

8.6.b

What did you _____ do?

Name _____

Dictated Phrases *just* and *rust*

1. _____

_____

2. _____

_____

3. _____

_____

Name _____

Review *u*__ Rimes in
Rime Family Words

Real Words	Non-Words

Name _____

Unit Rime Family Words

n<u>ut</u>

b<u>ug</u>

r<u>un</u>

d<u>uck</u>

r<u>ub</u>

j<u>ust</u>

Name _____

"Duck, Duck!"

The duck is a madcap nut.

She digs mad hats and just has fun.

She sees a nut and rubs it.

Out pops a bug! The bug is mad.
The duck bugged the bug.

The duck is in a jam.
She kicks the nut.

The duck runs, but…

DUCK!

Time taken:

1st reading _____ 2nd reading _____ 3rd reading _____

Name _____

Ender Bender Worksheet

Core Word	s	ing	ed	er
bug		bugging		x
run			ran	
rub			rubbed	
duck				
dip		dipping		x

Name _____

Words to Fit in Rhymes

Rhyme 1

luck   rug

Rhyme 2

run   fun   dust

Rhyme 3

tug   rusty   dusty

Rhyme 4

shut   bug

Name _____

Write Core Words With Ender Benders Worksheet 1

Core Word: _____

I will _____ it.

I am _____ it.

Yesterday, I _____ it.

I am a good _____!

· ·

Core Word: _____

I will _____ it.

I am _____ it.

Yesterday, I _____ it.

I am a good _____!

Name _____

Write Core Words With Ender Benders Worksheet 2

Core Word: _____

I will _____ it.

I am _____ it.

Yesterday, I _____ it.

I am a good _____!

• •

Core Word: _____

I will _____ it.

I am _____ it.

Yesterday, I _____ it.

I am a good _____!

Name _____

"Dan Is Napping"

Mom said, "Dan is napping. Do not bug him!"

So I sat with Dan and I rocked, but that did not bug Dan. Dan napped.

I tapped his rubber duck on the rug, but that did not bug Dan. Dan napped.

Then I had to run to see if Mom got in the van. But that did not bug Dan. Dan napped.

The cat was sitting on a nut, so I had to pick it up. That bugged the cat, but it did not bug Dan. Dan napped.

Then I rubbed his hand a little, and that bugged Dan!

So I hugged Dan.

Time taken:

1st reading _____ 2nd reading _____ 3rd reading _____

Name _____

RAN Chart (Core Words)

bug	nut	rub	run
duck	just	rub	nut
run	duck	just	bug

Time taken:

1st reading _____   2nd reading _____   3rd reading _____

Name _____

RAN Chart (Core Words + Review)

bug	top	dig	can
nut	lap	kick	rock
run	duck	hop	just

Time taken:

1st reading _____   2nd reading _____   3rd reading _____

Find the Verbs in "Dan Is Napping"

Mom said, "Dan is napping. Do not bug him!"

So I sat with Dan and I rocked, but that did not bug Dan. Dan napped.

I tapped his rubber duck on the rug, but that did not bug Dan. Dan napped.

Then I had to run to see if Mom got in the van. But that did not bug Dan. Dan napped.

The cat was sitting on a nut, so I had to pick it up. That bugged the cat, but it did not bug Dan. Dan napped.

Then I rubbed his hand a little, and that bugged Dan!

So I hugged Dan.

. . . .

1. Ender Bender **ed** on the end of a verb means: *it is happening now* or *it happened before today.*

   Highlight the one you think **ed** means.

2. The verbs that end in Ender Bender **ing** have the helping verbs

   _____ and _____ .

   Write the two helping verbs on the blank lines.

Name _____

Ticket Out the Door

The tap is running.

The bug in the cap runs.

The bug runs on the nut
in the dish.

The bug runs in the cap.

Name _____

Rime Family Words in Lesson 6

Real Words	Non-Words

Name _____

Make Your Own Sentences

Use this sheet to glue on the sentences you have made.

1. _____

   _____

2. _____

   _____

3. _____

   _____

4. _____

   _____

5. _____

   _____